A souvenir guide

Box Hill

Surrey

National Trust

An Iconic Landmark

Box Hill is one of the most cherished landmarks of south east England. Situated on the high chalk hills of the North Downs, and affording breathtaking views over the surrounding countryside, it is a strikingly beautiful example of English downland scenery.

Its characteristic broad-buttressed slopes form a bastion at the entrance to one of the few gaps along the backbone of the North Downs that otherwise lie largely unbroken from the Hampshire border to the White Cliffs of Dover. Through this gap, and below the time-worn precipitous river cliffs, flow the soft running waters of the River Mole, draining the Wealden lowlands to the south, away to the River Thames in the north.

Box Hill's archaeological history is still visible in places and includes two Bronze Age round barrows (*c.*2,500–700 BC), traces of a Celtic field system, the Roman road (Stane Street) which passes over Mickleham Downs, and the remains of medieval rabbit warrens.

Above Looking down the Zig Zag Road

Right Cowslips in April

Opposite 'I can see for miles and miles'

Below Enjoying the snow

A Hill for Enjoyment

Over the generations Box Hill has provided the perfect setting for recreation and relaxation. Whilst times have changed since the first tourists visited the Hill in the eighteenth century, its charm and unique appeal remains unchallenged, attracting hikers and dog-walkers, picknickers, cyclists, horse-riders, day trippers, and those interested in wildlife. Younger visitors flock to the Natural Play Trail which has transformed the Hill's natural features and materials into an exciting challenge.

Above Visitors enjoying a day out at Box Hill, 1929

Left Box Hill by motor bus, by Walter E. Spradbery, 1921

In August 1655 John Evelyn wrote of Box Hill:

'There were such goodly walkers and hills shaded with yew as render the place extreamely agreeable'.

By the late eighteenth century the growing metropolis of London fuelled a wave of day-trippers and visitors eager to escape the bustling smoky capital and soak up the clean air of the Downs. The growth of the turnpike road system and the expanding stagecoach service put Box Hill within easy reach of the city.

The arrival of the railway and Box Hill's own railway station in the mid-nineteenth century brought day trippers, walkers and sightseers to the foot of the Hill.

By Whit Monday in 1947 so popular was the Hill with Londoners for walking, cycling and picnicking that 14,000 visitors arrived at Box Hill station; the Hill was fondly in the hearts of locals and Londoners alike, keen to stretch their legs, breathe the fresh air and enjoy the countryside.

BOXHILL
BY MOTOR BUS

"...... the gorse-lit shoulder of the down
That keeps the north-wind from the nestling town."

GENERAL

Right **On the top of the world**

Below **Campers on Box Hill enjoy outdoor dancing in the early 1930s**

'On Sundays in the Afternoon the Company generally go to a charming Place called Box-Hill, about six Miles off where there is no House, but Arbors cut out in Box-Wood on the Top of the Hill, and there you may have for your Money all manner of Refreshments; and it's very easy for Gentlemen and Ladies insensibly to lose their Company in these pretty Labyrinths of Box-Woody and divert themselves unperceived. From hence one hath a most delicious commanding Prospect of fine Country, and it may be justly called the Palace of Venus.'

John Mackay, *A Journey Through England: In Familiar Letters*, Volume 1, 1714

Above Having fun on the Natural Play Trail

Right Cycling on Box Hill, 1934

The invention of the 'safety' cycle in 1894 heralded the start of a new chapter for Box Hill. As cycling mania took hold of an eager public, the Hill became a popular destination for any self-respecting cyclist, keen to pit his fitness against the heart-pumping climbs, and test his nerve on the jaw-dropping descents.

This special association with the Hill, experienced by generations of cyclists, continues to the present day. In 1875 Stanley Boorer caused quite a stir in the locality. Riding his clanking velocipede or 'bone shaker' from Denbies to Dorking in the dark and with glow worms attached to his hat, he frightened the returning housemaids out of their wits!

A tramping ground

In the late 1800s a group known as the Sunday Tramps would hike around Box Hill on fast-paced walks of up to 25-miles (40km), normally finishing with a mad dash for the last train back to London for supper. The tramps included retired mountaineers, politicians, intellectuals, writers and businessmen. As they walked they would discuss the topics of the day.

Let's go fly a kite

Box Hill is a great place for kite flying. Strong uplifts of air, open expanses and panoramic views provide the perfect 'sky-scape' for kite flyers.

Left Up, up and away

Below Miss Rachel Fardon riding a donkey on Box Hill, aged 6

A birthday treat

'Box Hill has very special childhood memories for me because of "Donkey Brown" who – in the 1920s and early 1930s – gave donkey rides on the large grassy area opposite the look-out. My main request for a treat (e.g. on my birthdays) was a donkey ride; this cost 3d. for a "there-and-back" distance, or 6d. for the whole way round the grassy area. In the evenings, the donkeys were brought down to the foot of Box Hill and were turned out in a field beside the A25, just to the east of the Watermill.'

Miss Rachel B. Fardon, 2010

Above **A family walk**

'A smooth lawn of grass, semi-circled by the wood, and looking down upon soft heathery slopes, and out upon far hills fitting in with farther hills; cool glades opening into the skirting leafage, into which those who will may wander off when the meal is done, while those who will may lie at length in a pleasing languor, and enjoy the view … the maidens busy themselves with the cloth-laying and the setting of knives and forks, also with the arrangement of the eatables, which the boys, for their part, help out of the rifled hampers, unpacking, with much relish, cold pies, chickens, lobsters, salad, ham, eggs, what not. Bottled Bass, sherry, claret … ice in flannel, and some soda water, not even omitting a few borage-leaves. Buddy cherries, and early apricots, and late strawberries, and blooming grapes … cold chicken and raspberry and currant tart, not to speak of etceteras.'

London Society, (1876)

The great outdoors

One of the greatest pleasures of a visit to Box Hill is to enjoy a picnic in beautiful surroundings. The word 'picnic' in the mid-eighteenth century referred to 'a fashionable social entertainment in which each person contributed a share of the provisions'. These events typically took place inside rather than out of doors and it was not until the early 1800s that the fashion for eating out in the countryside became popular.

Box Hill was the setting of the picnic scenes from the television series *Emma* (2008), based on the novel by Jane Austen:

Emma had never been to Box Hill; she wished to see what everybody found so well worth seeing.

A scene from *Emma*, 1996

The Olympic Games Cycle Road Race

By the 1890s Dorking Cycle Club was hosting cycle camps which were attended by hundreds of cyclists from the south east. Box Hill and the surrounding countryside offered the perfect place for outings, tours and endurance events.

Above Cyclists smiling happily in 1948

Right Olympic road race practice event

Above The men's cycle road race

Competition events such as road races, hill climbs and time trials soon became a regular part of the cycling calendar on and around the Hill and have continued to this day, ignited by the Olympic fever of the cycle road races.

Pedal to the medal: the men

For two days in July 2012 a special event took place at Box Hill. After two years of planning, ideas became reality as Surrey and Box Hill hosted the first event of the London 2012 Olympic Games.

The much vaunted men's cycle road race had been tipped from the start to be the launch pad for Mark Cavendish, the 'Manx Missile', to take the gold medal. Mark and Bradley Wiggins (fresh from winning the coveted yellow jersey in the Tour de France),

and their team mates Chris Froome, David Millar and Ian Stannard, stole the show. They were cheered on by 15,000 spectators on Box Hill plus hundreds of thousands of other supporters who lined the route from the Mall, through south-west London and out to the beautiful rolling Surrey countryside. Despite working hard over the 155-mile (250km) circuit, including nine climbs up Box Hill's Zig Zag road, they allowed the breakaway group to get too far ahead and medal places became a distant dream. The winners were:

Gold medal	Alexandr Vinokurov, Kazakhstan
Silver medal	Rigoberto Urán Urán, Columbia
Bronze medal	Alexander Kristoff, Norway

Pedal to the medal: the women

The next day, following the glorious sunshine of the opening race, the skies darkened as the GB ladies team comprising of Nicole Cooke, Lizzie Armitstead, Emma Pooley and Lucy Martin made their way up the Zig Zag on the first of their two hill climbs. Heavy thunder and rain welcomed the home team as they neared the summit of the Hill, but their spirits must have been warmed by the thousands of spectators who had braved the English summer rain to cheer the cyclists on. The weather though was 'pure Yorkshire' for Lizzie Armitstead, Team GB's hopeful, as she powered her way up Box Hill, leaving her fellow cyclists far behind. Staying in the leading group for the entire race ultimately made Lizzie a very delighted and proud silver-medal winner.

Above Olympic road race practice event

Gold medal	Marianne Voss, Netherlands
Silver medal	Lizzie Armitstead, Great Britain
Bronze medal	Olga Zabelinskaya, Russia

A special climb

'Box Hill will always be a special climb for me as I associate it with my success at the Olympics. The gradient isn't too steep which makes it a great place to practise basic skills like using your gears and developing good bike control whilst also challenging your fitness. The best bit about Box Hill is that it offers some of the best views of the Surrey Hills, and there is a café at the top to reward yourself after the climb!'

Lizzie Armitstead, silver medallist, London Olympics 2012

Right Cycling over Richard Long's 'Road River'

A site of Special Scientific Interest

The sporting achievement of the athletes isn't the only triumphant part of this story however. Box Hill is a Site of Special Scientific Interest (SSSI) and a Special Area of Conservation (SAC), as well as forming an integral part of the Surrey Hills Area of Outstanding Natural Beauty (AONB). It is because of these designations and the sheer number of spectators, that this becomes a very remarkable story.

To balance the needs of conservation and play host to a global cycling event was always going to be a challenge. Working closely with Natural England (the statutory advisor for the UK government), areas were set aside where spectators could safely watch the race alongside the rare flora and fauna. Dormice, orchids and butterflies were most at threat from large crowds trampling the fragile environment. Fortunately the post-Olympic bio-survey has revealed that no lasting damage was caused, proving that access and conservation can exist side by side if managed correctly.

Above The Olympic rings

Below Butterfly art on the Zig Zag road

Right Crowds watching the big screen

Opposite below Supporting Team GB

H. Shackleton 2012

A world-wide audience

With a world-wide television audience of around two billion watching the Olympic cycle road races, it was important to share the excitement and significance of Box Hill. New welcome signs were erected, the visitor centre was painted, new toilets were installed and the Box Tree Café sprang up, created out of the old shop. The Adonis blue butterfly was brought vividly to life on the Hill as three giant paintings by artist Helen Shackleton were applied as transfers onto the road, reminding spectators of the beauty of the natural world. Standing proudly over all this were the 48-feet (14m) high Olympic rings which dazzled in the summer sunshine and looked over Dorking and the surrounding countryside.

Graffiti

One of the legacies of the Olympic cycle road races was Box Hill's joint venture with Turner prize-winning artist, Richard Long. Famed for his work in the outdoors, and a keen cyclist and walker, Richard seized on the opportunity to create a work for the London 2012 Olympic festival. The 'Box Hill Road River' is the outcome of several site visits and was inspired by the bends of the Zig Zag road, the chalk landscape of Box Hill and the tradition of leaving messages on the road to encourage cyclists. At over 100 yards (91m) long, the sinuous white work which was created in just one night, lies proudly on the Hill, a permanent reminder of the toil, joy and anguish of 28 and 29 July 2012.

Curiosities of the Hill

The Hill's breathtaking views and natural wonders have inspired writers, scientists and composers through the centuries.

A holm oak tree is growing up through the tower but was not planted there intentionally. It is most likely that the acorn was dropped in by a passing bird. Jays are commonly seen at Box Hill and love eating and hiding acorns.

Broadwood's Tower

Thomas Broadwood was the son of John Broadwood, the founder of a company which made pianos. In 1818 Thomas visited Beethoven in Vienna and sent him a six-octave grand piano that was later owned by the composer Liszt. In the early nineteenth century Thomas lived at nearby Juniper Hall and built a circular flint tower known as Broadwood's Folly on the crest of Lodge Hill.

Broadwood's Tower has most recently been celebrated by Surrey's largest vineyard, Denbies. To celebrate the Queen's Diamond Jubilee and the 2012 Olympics the company have produced a sparkling wine called Broadwood's Folly.

Opposite Broadwood's Tower

Right Major Peter Labilliere

A walking 'dung-hill'

In the late eighteenth century Major Peter Labilliere, a marine officer, lived close to Box Hill. By all accounts a gentle and sensitive soul, his life was marked by a number of eccentricities. He frequently walked to London, followed by a tribe of ragged boys, whom he would occasionally harangue, both his pockets being generally filled, to an overflow, with newspapers and political pamphlets. His inattention to cleanliness earned him the name 'the walking dung-hill'. Perhaps his greatest eccentricity was his last request: to be buried upside-down at his favourite haunt on Box Hill. His burial is commemorated on the north-western brow of the Hill where a stone marks his grave. During the burial someone stole the wooden bridge over the River Mole and the mourners had to wade through the river or take a lengthy detour home.

Taking to the air

Not content with walking and cycling on the Hill, in 1910 a young engineer called John Turnbull designed and built a small glider near the top of Box Hill. With a framework of bamboo, braced with wire and covered with sailcloth, the glider was flown as a hang-glider controlled by the pilot shifting the weight of his body. Take-off was aided by a four-wheel trolley propelled down the steep slope of the Hill.

A topsy-turvy world
Major Peter Labilliere was buried with his head downwards; it being a constant assertion with him, 'that the world was turned topsy-turvy, and, therefore, at the end of it he should be right'.

Extract from Peter Labilliere's *The Man Buried Upside Down on Box Hill*, by James Lander, 2000

A breath of fresh air

The poet and novelist George Meredith (1828–1909) lived at Flint Cottage, situated at the foot of Box Hill, for more than 40 years. He was deeply touched by the immense natural beauty of his surroundings, an empathy which imprinted an everlasting influence on his work and life. You can see the wooden chalet where he did much of his writing from an area of the Burford Spur known as Barrie's Bank, named after J.M. Barrie, the author of Peter Pan. Barrie paid many visits to Box Hill to visit his friend Meredith, and his writing was inspired by the

'I am every morning at the top of Box Hill – as its flower, its bird, its prophet. I drop down the moon on one side, I draw up the sun on t'other. I breathe fine air. I shout 'ha ha' to the gates of the world. Then I descend and know myself a donkey for doing it.'

George Meredith, 1868

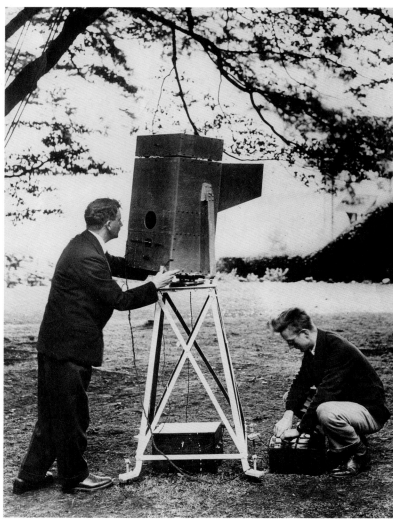

Above George Meredith's writing chalet at Box Hill

Opposite Caricature of George Meredith, drawn by Max Beerbohm, 1896

Above right John Logie Baird and his Noctovisor – 'A machine for seeing by wireless'

serenity of the Hill. Others who made the pilgrimage to Flint Cottage included George Gissing and Henry James, as well as the critic and caricaturist Max Beerbohm who lived there for a time during the Second World War.

Roll ... camera ... action!

In 1930 the television pioneer John Logie Baird conducted some of his early experiments at Swiss Cottage, a flint house on the summit of Box Hill. He lived here between 1929 and 1932 and used its high vantage point to send signals to the valley below.

One of his demonstrations at Box Hill was the 'Noctovisor', a device which relied on infrared light as illumination for television. His first experiments with infrared used electric fires and on one occasion a dummy actually burst into flames. His successful infrared source turned out to be an ordinary light bulb coated with ebonite to block visible radiation.

Fighting Talk

Brighton has fallen! … The invaders have reached Horsham! … Stand to your arms volunteers! … Now then, gentlemen, give it them hot!

Extracts taken from *The Battle of Dorking*, by General Sir George Chesney, 1861

Standing sentry over the market town of Dorking and forming a natural blockade between the south coast of England and London, Box Hill Fort is a stark reminder of the threat posed to London by the French at the end of the eighteenth century. 'The serene and peaceful surroundings of Box Hill became the scene of a desperate and unsuccessful attempt by a ramshackle English army to repel enemy forces on their way to

capturing London.' Or so wrote General Sir George Chesney in *Blackwood's Magazine*, 1861, in an attempt to show the military authorities how vulnerable England would be from an attack by an invading army.

Inside the fort the narrow passages which led into the magazines where the ammunition was stored were lit by oil lamps. To prevent the danger of sparks flying, the volunteers had to wear special felt slippers.

Above Box Hill Fort

Opposite Cut-away drawing of the Fort

Chesney's alarming essay did not go unnoticed by General Sir Edward Hamley, a leading campaigner for better defences against a possible invasion from the Continent. His proposal for a line of lightly fortified assembly points around London was taken seriously by the Government and in 1888 a scheme was given the go-ahead. This included the construction of 12 military installations in a line from Guildford to Knockholt known as The London Defence Scheme, a last ditch line of 'forts' to protect the capital.

Just over 5 acres (2 hectares) of land were bought on the top of Box Hill for the construction of a fortified structure. Costing £8,584 for land purchase and works, the concrete defences were completed by 1900, serving as a mobilisation base and supply depot for regular soldiers and volunteers. But within ten years of completion military strategy had changed: as confidence in supremacy of the Royal Navy was restored with the launch of HMS *Dreadnought*, the fastest and most heavily armoured battleship ever built. Such changes marked the end for Hamley's scheme which was now no longer required. The costly 'white elephant' at Box Hill was sold back to the original owners in 1908.

Bats

Today the concrete defences are home to a rather different 'garrison battery' of the Hill. Three different species of bat – the brown long-eared bat, the noctule bat and Natterer's bat – inhabit the old fort, thriving in the damp rooms and cool, constant temperatures. Look out for them at dusk as they start their nightly foraging activities over the hillsides and woods.

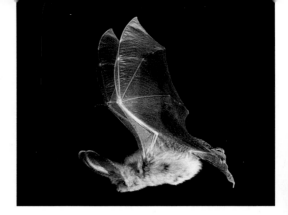

Above Brown long-eared bat

Left Noctule bat

Above Women cutting wood for use in munitions in the Second World War

Opposite A Type 24 infantry shell-proof pill box situated close to the River Mole.

The Second World War

There are several remains of Second World War installations on Box Hill including a Type 24 infantry shell-proof pill box and tank traps.

Wartime memories

I was eight when the war started and I have lots of memories of different events during those years:

I remember sitting on the Viewpoint with my parents watching the Doodle Bugs going over, there were so many of them going so fast that we didn't go to school that day or several others as well. We even saw two or three Doodle Bugs shot down. One of the craters at the side of the Zig-Zag is from a Doodle Bug or a bomb I can't remember which it was now.

As well as the doodle bugs we saw planes having dog fights during the Battle of Britain which was very exciting. Another day a bomb crater appeared in the woods out of the blue … during the evacuation from Dunkirk we went to Box Hill Farm to watch all the people on the trains being evacuated. There were no civilian trains for a couple of weeks. This caused real problems for people trying to get to work in London.

Before D Day we used to sit on the Burford Spur and watch the A24 between Mickleham & Dorking filled with tanks and other army vehicles as they used it as a staging area. They used to wash vehicles in the River Mole by the Stepping Stones. During those war years we saw the tank traps on the River Mole and three pill boxes being built on the Hill as possible defences. As I see them still there today it brings back all these memories as if it was yesterday.

Peter Downing, 2010

Geology

Box Hill forms part of the North Downs which are made of chalk and were formed millions of years ago as layer upon layer of microscopic organisms fell to the sea bed when the area was covered by ocean.

Over millions of years, the sea and land levels changed to leave the chalk and surrounding rocks exposed to the elements. Sandstones and clays were worn away by frost, rain and ice to leave the escarpments and hills that we know as the North and South Downs.

The River Mole runs along the foot of Box Hill. It is a great place to get away from the hustle and bustle and take in the peace and serenity of the river's own pace of life.

There are different stories behind the name of the Mole. One belief is that it comes from the burrowing animal as some stretches of the river flow underground during dry periods.

The Stepping Stones

Seventeen hexagonal stepping stones cross the River Mole at the foot of Box Hill. The crossing point marks the line of an ancient route-way running the length of the North Downs from Hampshire to the Straits of Dover. The stones were removed during the Second World War to prevent invading forces crossing the river. They were replaced in 1946, when they were dedicated by the then Prime Minister, Clement Attlee.

If you are lucky you might catch a glimpse of a kingfisher darting past, like a bolt of blue lightning.

Above **The Stepping Stones in the 1940s**

Right **Kingfisher**

Opposite **The Stepping Stones today**

Flora and Fauna

Box Hill is treasured for its native animals and plants. The special type of grassland which thrives on the chalk soils is known as downland and is packed full of an awesome array of wildflowers and grasses and insects, rich in sight, sound and smell.

Downland

Since earliest times woodland clearance over the chalk hills have created a natural habitat called chalk downland. This is a springy turf of differing heights which, because of the thin soils beneath, creates perfect conditions for small flowers and herbs where no plant dominates. This delicate balance supports as many as 40 plant species per square metre. In amongst the low growing wild strawberry and rockrose, spring up the spikes of over a dozen rare orchids – the man, the fragrant and the bee orchid to name just three, and all about there are fragrant wafts of wild marjoram, thyme and basil. Truly a wonderful place to take your rest – an ant's tussock, your pillow!

Woodland

Just a few short strides away from wherever you are on Box Hill you are close to the woods. Famous of course for box, a short evergreen shrub which grows almost everywhere on Box Hill, you can also find yourself in amongst the

Highly valued

Boxwood is particularly good for fine carving because of its hardness and was commonly used to make blocks for wood engravings. It was also highly prized for parts of musical pipes and flutes, carpenter's rules, mathematical instruments, furniture inlays, munitions and chessmen.

twisted stems and dark leaves of groves of yew which send out clouds of smoke-like pollen in spring, and bears poisonous seeds later in the year. Largely the woods are left alone to complete the natural cycle of seeding, growth, death and decay – each part of the lifecycle helping our natural wildlife to thrive.

Opposite Lodge Hill

Below Engraving of a whimbrel, from *The History of British Birds*, 1797, by Thomas Bewick, with the original boxwood block

Insects

Because of its flowers, Box Hill is home to a great array of insects; the chirring grasshoppers and the shiny gleam of beetles join the darting and fluttering brilliance of over 40 different species of butterfly and many more moths. Two real specialities are the rather drab straw belle moth, classified as rare in the UK Biodiversity Action Plan, and the Adonis blue butterfly which has a special relationship with the yellow meadow ant and the horseshoe vetch plant.

Above Adonis blue butterfly

Left Six-spot burnet moths on a spear thistle

The caterpillar will only eat the leaves of this vetch so that is where the butterfly lays her eggs. The ants then take the caterpillar into their nest and give it protection – in return it gives them a sweet sticky fluid, after which the pupa lives in the nest finally crawling out as an adult – now that's natures magic.

Protecting our wildlife

Managing Box Hill as a place for fun, wildlife and beautiful scenery is a full-time job. A team of dedicated countryside rangers and an impressive band of volunteers get to grips with a range of jobs from livestock management to litter picking.

You may see the belted Galloway cattle out on the Hill keeping our chalk downland turf short or tussocky and munching a bit of woody scrub along the way – it's a natural way of keeping the habitat in good shape and we want them here for ever. Humans help them sometimes, cutting areas that they cannot manage, have left alone, or do not like to go.

Below **Belted Galloway** cattle

Right **Dormouse** hibernating

Headley Heath

The wide expanse of Headley Heath to the east of Box Hill, provides the perfect place for enjoying one of Surrey's heathland commons. The open views and drier ground are ideal for horse riding, dog walking and getting a spot of fresh air.

In the past, heathlands such as Headley Heath covered vast tracts of southern England, providing an important subsistence resource for rural farming communities. Many of these 'commons' were used as shared grazing areas between neighbouring villages. Before the end of the nineteenth century Headley Heath was used for grazing sheep from the parishes of Betchworth, Brockham and Headley. The villagers also used heather, gorse and turf to make fires and provide animal bedding.

Grazing ceased at Headley Heath after the area was requisitioned by the army for tank training during the Second World War. After the war the open character of the common began to change. Bracken, birch and bramble quickly colonised many areas at the expense of heathland plants.

In 1946 the National Trust acquired Headley Heath and began to restore the heath. In recent years cattle have been reintroduced to continue the restoration work. Results are encouraging for birds; woodlark, nightjar and Dartford warbler have returned after an absence of many years. The heath is also a nationally important site for starfruit which grows in the cattle-poached pond edges, and bears seed pods of six-pointed stars.

The dry sandy and gravelly soils characteristic of Headley, allow acid-loving plants such as the ling and bell heathers and gorse to thrive. At Headley Heath chalky soils also come to the surface on the valley slopes, giving rise to the rare 'chalk heath' habitat where chalk downland plants live side by side with acid-loving plants.

to Box Hill →
via Box Hill Hike Markers

9

P

to Walton →

Below **Starfruit flowers**
Below right **Headley Heath**

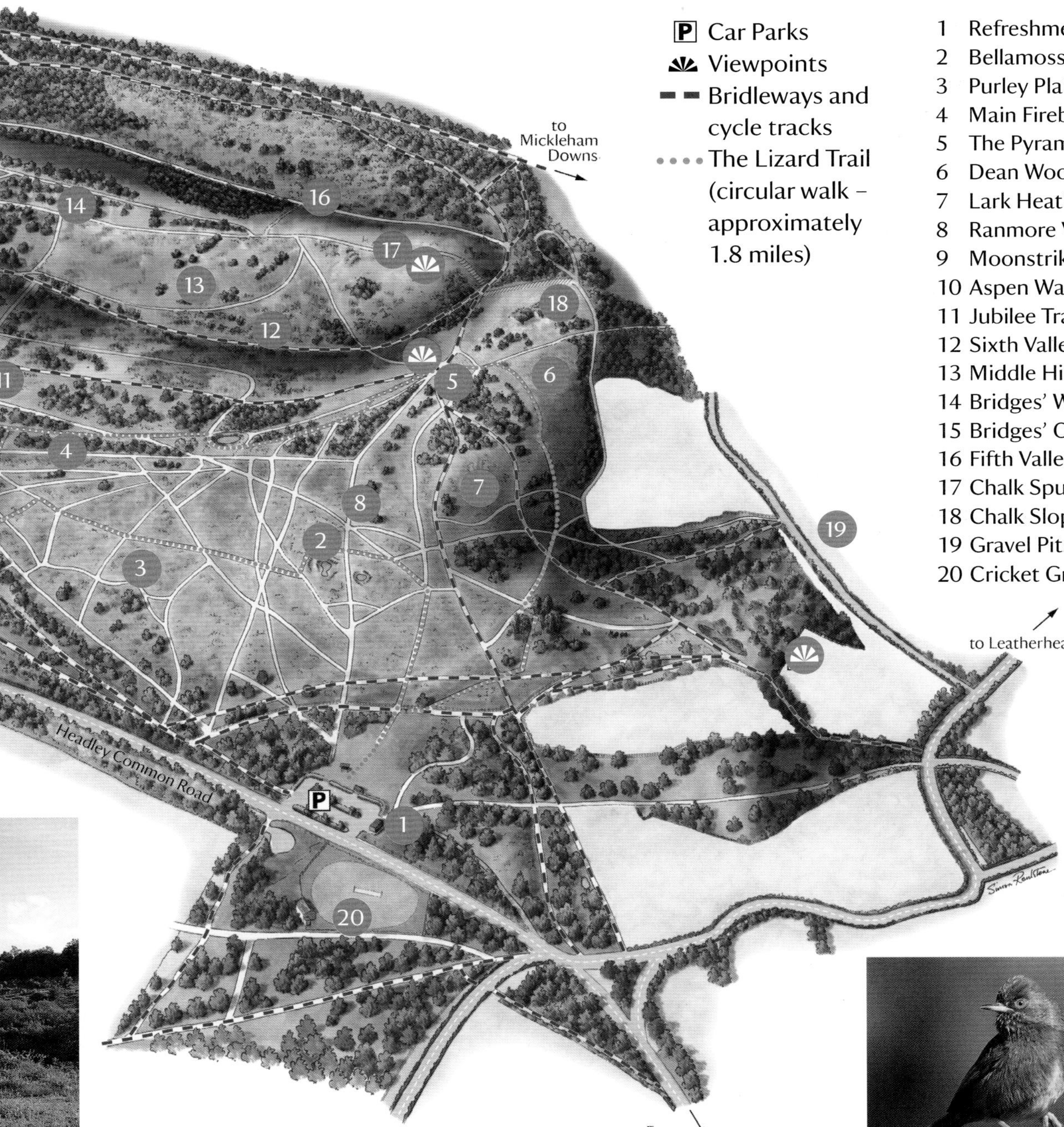
to
Mickleham
Downs
Headley Common Road
to Leatherhead
to Epsom
P
1
2
3
4
5
6
7
8
11
12
13
14
16
17
18
19
20

P Car Parks
Viewpoints
Bridleways and cycle tracks
The Lizard Trail (circular walk – approximately 1.8 miles)

1 Refreshment kiosk
2 Bellamoss Pond
3 Purley Plain
4 Main Firebreak
5 The Pyramids
6 Dean Wood Heath
7 Lark Heath
8 Ranmore Vista
9 Moonstrike Cross
10 Aspen Walk
11 Jubilee Track
12 Sixth Valley Track
13 Middle Hill
14 Bridges' Walk
15 Bridges' Oaks
16 Fifth Valley Track
17 Chalk Spur
18 Chalk Slope
19 Gravel Pits
20 Cricket Ground

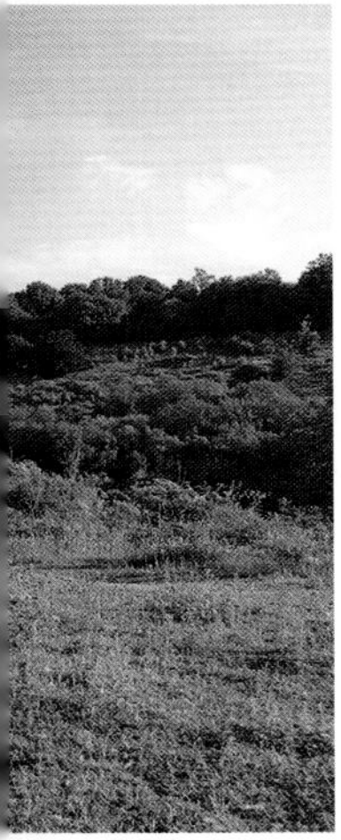

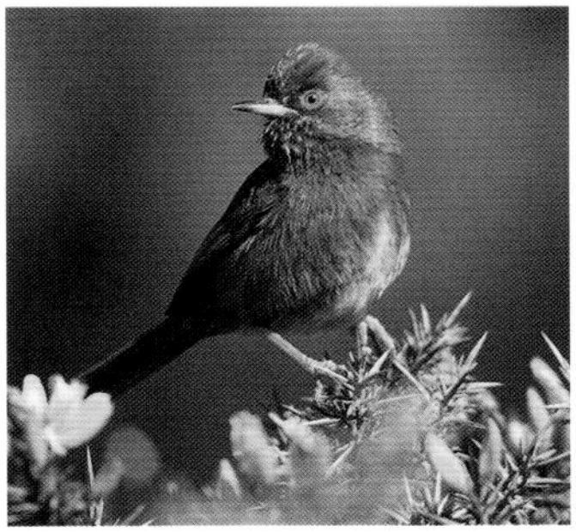

Dartford warbler on a gorse plant

A Lasting Legacy

In 1912, 232 acres (94 hectares) of Box Hill were offered for sale on the open market. Leopold Salomons of nearby Norbury Park purchased the land for £16,000 and donated it to the National Trust in 1914. Since then further purchases, legacies and donations have seen the National Trust land around Box Hill expand to some 1,210 acres (490 hectares).

Today, a group called the Friends of Box Hill support the property in a range of different ways including raising much-needed funds while the day to day management is carried out by the National Trust's dedicated countryside management team.

Peace and fresh air, a place to walk the dog, run through autumn leaves, splash in puddles and enjoying a reviving flapjack at the end of a steep cycle climb are just some of the things that make Box Hill so special. Everyone has a different reason for their visit and that's why we work hard to look after this wonderful place – for ever, for everyone.

Above **A living sculpture**